JOHN KINROSS

Discovering
Scottish
Battlefields

SHIRE PUBLICATIONS LTD

CONTENTS

The cover illustration is a detail from a lithograph of about 1840, 'The Field of Preston Pans'.

Copyright © 1976 and 1986 by John Kinross. Number 174 in the 'Discovering' series. ISBN 0 85263 750 0. First published 1976 as 'Discovering Battlefields of Scotland', second edition 1986. (The descriptions of Bannockburn, Dunbar, Prestonpans and Culloden first published 1968 in 'Discovering Battlefields in Northern England and Scotland.')

INTRODUCTION

Scottish battles are many and various. Clan fought against clan before Scots fought English. This book does not attempt to list all the battles. It includes those that I have studied closely and whose sites I have visited. If more attention is given to Montrose and the Jacobite rebellions it is because they are a constant source of wonder. How could a great leader succeed in so many battles and yet lose one in which he made mistakes which were elementary? What made Charles fail to follow up his success at Falkirk? Why did Monmouth succeed at Bothwell Bridge, only to lose six years later at Sedgemoor? These are some of the questions that arise from the battles described.

Sources are numerous, but special mention should be made of J. Robson's articles in *The Border magazine,* volume II (1897), *The battle of Sheriffmuir,* published by Eneas Mackay of Stirling (1898). Andrew Lang's *History of Scotland,* volumes I-IV (1907), and P. Hume Brown's *History of Scotland,* volumes I-III (1912).

Special thanks are due to Mr H. Hanley and the staff of the Buckinghamshire County Record Office, who turned up a letter in the Trevor Papers describing Falkirk; to Mr D. N. Struan Robertson and his son for information on the Robertson banner; to the National Trust for Scotland, which sets so fine an example in its care of Auldearn, Bannockburn, Culloden and Killiecrankie; to Mr C. d'O. Pilkington Jackson, sculptor of the equestrian statue of Robert Bruce at Bannockburn, for information about the statue and this and other battles; and to Leiutenant-Colonel I. B. Cameron Taylor BSc, FSA (Scotland), formerly Historian to the National Trust for Scotland, for his invaluable advice.

The map reference in each heading refers to the sheet number of the Ordnance Survey 1:50,000 series.

ACKNOWLEDGEMENTS

Photographs are acknowledged as follows: the Scottish Tourist Board, plates 1, 2, 3, 6, 8, 9; Brian Shuel, plate 7. Plates 4 and 5 are by the author. The cover picture is reproduced by courtesy of the National Army Museum. The battle plans are by Shirley Barker.

▭	Foot soldiers
◿	Cavalry
——	Roads existing now and at time of battle
- - -	Roads built since time of battle

Key to the battle plans

3

LOCATIONS OF BATTLES

1 Alford
2 Ancrum Moor
3 Auldearn
4 Bannockburn
5 Bothwell Bridge
6 Culloden

7 Dunbar
8 Falkirk
9 Glen Shiel
10 Harlaw
11 Killiecrankie
12 Kilsyth

13 Langside
14 Philiphaugh
15 Pinkie
16 Prestonpans
17 Sheriffmuir
18 Stirling Bridge

STIRLING BRIDGE,
11th September 1297

Central O/S 57 (784 950)

The death of Alexander III, King of Scots, in 1286 left the Scottish succession in doubt. There were two main contenders for the throne, Robert Bruce and John Balliol, his cousin. In England Edward I naturally preferred the weaker man, and in 1292 Balliol was declared king. He promptly did homage to Edward, who became ruler in all but name. When Scotland was asked to supply troops to defend Gascony, Balliol objected and in 1295 he signed a peace treaty with the French court.

In 1296 Balliol surrendered Scotland to Edward without the acquiescence of the Scots. The Earl of Surrey was appointed governor of the country or in reality, of the English garrisons, and his treasurer was Hugh Cressingham. In times of crisis Scotland always seems to produce the right leader and in 1297 William Wallace, the second son of a little-known knight from Paisley who had been killed by the English, emerged as the leading patriot. He gathered an army with his friends Moray, Ramsay and Graham and besieged Dundee, which was in English hands. Cressingham and Surrey made for Stirling with a large army — some reports say fifty thousand, but it was probably less than half that number and it certainly outnumbered Wallace's.

Wallace doubled back at great speed from Dundee to hold the Forth crossing. The river was crossed by a single wooden bridge one mile upstream from the place where the old stone bridge stands today. The Scottish carpenters fixed the bridge so that it could be demolished by the quick removal of a single timber. Wallace then camped on Abbey Craig hill and awaited developments. Two Dominican friars were sent to Wallace by Surrey to make peace, but this was firmly refused. A Scottish knight in Edward's army — he had many Balliol supporters of doubtful reliability — volunteered to take some horse over the river by a nearby ford. Cressingham urged a simple crossing of the wooden bridge and, afraid of being superseded as Governor, Surrey agreed. All day the English filed over, forming up on the flat land opposite. At about eleven o'clock, seeing that half the troops were over, Wallace decided to attack. A party of Scots attacked from Cambuskenneth Abbey and held the Scottish side of the bridge. The English vanguard under Sir Marmaduke de Twenge charged the Scots as they descended but the Scottish archers caused havoc in the dense English ranks. Some reinforcements got across before the bridge collapsed and Sir Marmaduke was one of the few to escape, with some of his cavalry.

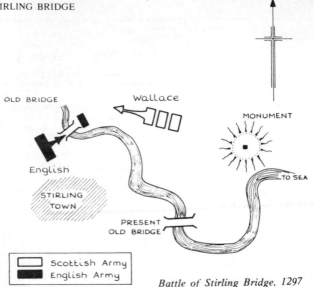

Battle of Stirling Bridge, 1297

Meanwhile the Scottish horse, about two hundred in number, had crossed by the ford and harried the English retreat. The English were driven to Berwick. Thousands were killed, including Treasurer Cressingham. Edward was forced to give up his plan but the following year he returned with a larger army and defeated Wallace at Falkirk.

Stirling Bridge today

The old bridge that exists at Stirling today next to the modern one dates from 1400 and is about a mile downstream from where the battle is supposed to have taken place. A visit to the Wallace Monument to see the displays and the lie of the land is useful.

BANNOCKBURN, 24th June 1314
Central O/S 57 (393 669)

The English victory at Dunbar in 1296 over the Scots, who had ousted Edward I's puppet king Balliol, was the beginning of the Scottish War of Independence. When Wallace was defeated two years later by Edward's army at Falkirk, the Scots looked to another leader, Robert Bruce. The tide of fortune turned slowly but in 1307 Edward I died and his successor Edward II was not the brilliant soldier his father had been. In March 1306 Bruce had disposed of his rival Comyn and crowned himself King of Scotland at Scone. Edward allowed the situation to deteriorate and by 1313 the English garrisons at Perth, Dumfries, Edinburgh and Roxburgh had surrendered, and Mowbray had agreed to surrender Stirling to Edward Bruce, Robert's brother, by Midsummer Day 1314 unless he was relieved by an English army.

The Scots arranged a gathering at Torwood near Stirling as Edward's army of twenty-two thousand marched through Edinburgh towards Stirling. Bruce's army was about eight thousand strong, of which five thousand were spearmen armed with twelve-foot spears and steel helmets, five hundred were lightly armed horsemen, and a few were archers. The Scots were in five groups under Edward and Robert Bruce, Douglas and Randolph Moray with Sir Robert Keith commanding the horsemen. The English knights were heavily armoured and their horses were weighed down by the impedimenta of an army on the march. Bruce withdrew his men to the New Park, a thick wood on the edge of the little river Bannock blocking the Falkirk-Stirling road. He dug concealed pits and covered the ground with calthrops — spikes to prevent the passage of horses — and then sat down to wait for his enemy.

The younger English knights, arriving at the Bannock on 23rd June, immediately pressed forward to attack the outnumbered Scots. Sir Humphrey Bohun spotted Bruce himself and drove his horse at him with his lance levelled. Dodging to one side, the king

Battle of Bannockburn, 1314 (first positions)

7

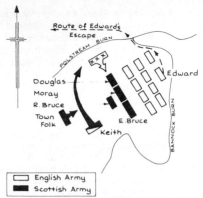

Battle of Bannockburn, 1314 (later positions)

of the Scots brought down his heavy axe and shattered both axe and Bohun's helmet with one mighty blow. The English vanguard withdrew demoralised. The Scots were exultant.

Early next morning the Scottish spearmen advanced in their densely packed formations called schiltrons. The English were in low-lying marshland between the Polstream and the Bannock burns. Edward hastily ordered his nephew the Duke of Gloucester and his horsemen to attack. The Scots had been trained to kill the horses first, so that the heavy English knights would be helpless. It was a cruelly effective plan and was used by the clansmen at Prestonpans four hundred years later. Young Gloucester was one of the first to fall and he was followed by Clifford, Sir Edmund de Mauley, Sir Pain Tiptoft and many other English knights. The English and Welsh archers, stationed at the rear, could do no damage. When they reached the flank, where they checked the spearmen for a time, Keith's horsemen cut them down.

The Scots were still outnumbered but many of the English could not reach the front ranks to fight. Suddenly a small army of townsfolk from Stirling entered the fray. Armed with home-made weapons and waving blanket banners, they cut off the stragglers. Edward, wielding his battleaxe, had his horse killed under him but was rescued by his bodyguard who took him safely to Dunbar and Berwick. One of them, Sir Giles d'Argentan, refused to escape and plunged his horse into the nearest schiltron. 'I am not accustomed to fly,' he said, 'nor shall I do so now.'

The flight of their king was the signal for panic. The English fled back through the Bannock where many were killed and trampled on. Several hundred were drowned in the Forth or killed by the country folk. Aylmer de Valence, Lord Pembroke, the man who had beaten Bruce at Methven eight years before, succeeded in escaping with the Welsh archers to Carlisle. Bruce was generous to his prisoners and let many go free. His own men were rewarded with the captured English spoil. A wheelwright from Stirling, a young man called Kinross, who was one of the last to arrive at the action, was granted land in the town. Mowbray, the governor of the castle, was received as a friend in Bruce's camp. Scotland had won her independence for a time and England had suffered her worst defeat since Hastings.

Bannockburn today

Bannockburn is a few miles south of Stirling on A80. Protected by the National Trust for Scotland, Bruce's position on the first day of the battle is now marked by a fine statue of the King of Scots mounted on his charger. The statue was made by C. d'O. Pilkington Jackson and unveiled by the Queen in 1964. The Heritage Centre nearby has an excellent audio-visual interpretation of the whole battle in its auditorium.

HARLAW, 24th July 1411

Grampian O/S 38 (752 242)

The final struggle for supremacy between the Highlands and the Lowlands took place about twenty miles north of Aberdeen. Harlaw today is forgotten by historians, yet it was one of the bloodiest battles ever fought between Scots. The death of King Robert III in 1406 and the capture of his son by the English left Scotland in the hands of the Duke of Albany. He was an ambitious statesman of considerable popularity, but he was tied to an English truce, for his own son was also a prisoner of Henry IV.

Donald, Lord of the Isles, the Celtic chieftain, demanded the earldom of Ross from Albany, but the latter refused as his own son had a better right to the earldom. In 1408, when Albany was turning to France, Donald made a treaty with Henry asking the English king to support his claim which would give him most of northern Scotland. Heading out from Ardtornish Castle on the Sound of Mull, Donald crossed to the mainland and augmented his force of islanders from the clans, mostly Macleans, Macleods, Camerons and the Clan Chattan. Brushing aside Angus Mackay's small force of northern clans, he assembled his ten thousand men at Inverness and promised them the free plunder of Aberdeen.

Fortunately for Aberdeen, the Earl of Mar, a son of the Wolf of Badenoch and a relation of the Lord of the Isles, was as great and brave a warrior as Donald and had fought in Flanders. With the support of the burgesses of Aberdeen he collected an army and marched out to meet Donald. Though hopelessly outnumbered,

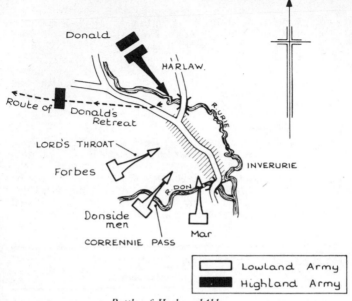

Battle of Harlaw, 1411

Mar's army was superior in mail-clad knights and they held their own all afternoon and all night. In the morning the clans had vanished and only the dead remained. So many were slain in this action that it became known as 'Red Harlaw'.

Albany followed up the retreating Celts, capturing their stronghold at Dingwall. Donald finally submitted to Albany at Lochgilp in Knapdale. In 1424, after Albany's death, the rightful king, James I of Scotland, returned in triumph to rule his country with an English bride, Lady Jane Beaufort. The canny Scots carefully deducted £10,000 dowry from their £40,000 ransom before the agreement was signed, a piece of diplomacy which must have appealed to both Highlanders and Lowlanders alike.

Harlaw today

A few miles north of Inverurie there is a large monument commemorating the battle. It is found by turning off the B9001 after it crosses the little river Urie.

Robert Davidson, Provost of Aberdeen, was killed leading a group of citizens at Harlaw. He was buried in the north wall of Saint Nicholas's church, Aberdeen, and the armour that can be seen in the entrance hall of Aberdeen's Town House is, according to tradition, his.

Henry VIII was especially bitter towards Scotland at the end of his reign. The Pope had appointed Archbishop Beaton of St Andrews as one of his cardinals and the Scots had rejected Henry's proposal of the marriage of his son Edward to the infant Mary, Queen of Scots. Apart from this, he was at war with France and could not afford to let the 'auld alliance' of France and Scotland develop.

The Earl of Hertford was sent to raid Scotland. 'Spoil and turn upside down the cardinal's town of St Andrews, as the upper stone may be the nether', went the instructions from the king, 'sparing no creature alive.' After landing at Leith, the English carried out these harsh orders and even pillaged Edinburgh. The weak Earl of Arran was not able to raise an army but in the borders the Earl of Angus, recently recalled from exile, had seen his estates ravaged by two English knights, Sir Ralph Evers and Sir Brian Latoun. In 1545 these two led an army of five thousand, of whom three thousand were foreign mercenaries and eight hundred broken Scottish clans, into Scotland by way of Jedburgh. Melrose Abbey was pillaged and the graves of the Douglases were desecrated. On his way back to Jedburgh by the Roman road Evers saw the Scottish army of Angus, Scott of Buccleuch and Leslie on Peniel Heugh, a fair-sized hill to the left of the road. He noticed their horse retreating and gave the order to attack. The English were overloaded with booty and, when they had struggled up the hill, they found the Scottish army in a hollow calmly awaiting the attack. The sun, wind and smoke from the arquebuses obscured the English banners so that the mercenaries did not know friend

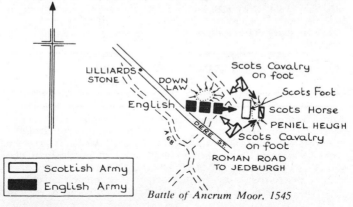

Battle of Ancrum Moor, 1545

11

from foe, especially as the eight hundred borderers changed sides and joined Angus's line.

Armed with the Jedburgh axe, a terrifying weapon consisting of a billhook on one side and a metal hook on the other, the Scots set upon the cavalry of Latoun and Bowes, pulling riders from their horses and stabbing them on the ground. With cries of 'Remember Broomhouse' the Scottish spearmen advanced. (Broomhouse was a tower burnt by the English with its lady and her family.) Latoun's cavalry fled through the second and third lines. Evers and Latoun were killed. Nearly a thousand men were captured and the Scottish losses were small. The town of Jedburgh was freed from the English, the wagon train was captured and the abbey of Coldingham, which had been fortified by the English, was regained. Ancrum was a decisive victory and one that helped to unify Scotland, for Angus had been under suspicion of being in the pay of Henry VIII. Henry had fresh worries, for in the summer of the same year, spurred on by the Scottish success, the French landed two thousand men in the Isle of Wight and Annebaut's fleet attacked Portsmouth.

Ancrum Moor today

The battlefield is simple to find because Peniel Heugh has a large Wellington monument on the top, visible from the A68 a few miles north of Jedburgh. On the line of the Roman road is the tomb of Maiden Lilliard, bearing the following inscription:

Fair maiden Lilliard lies under this stane,
Little was her stature, but muckle was her fame;
Upon the English loons she laid many thumps,
And when her legs were cuttit off,
She fought upon her stumps.

According to tradition Lilliard's lover had been killed by the English and she drove into their ranks with a sword, continuing to fight when her legs had been cut off by Evers's men.

The chapel-like building on Down Law has no connection with the battle.

PINKIE, 10th September 1547
Lothian O/S 66 (361 716)

In 1547 Henry VIII died and it was suggested that the young King Edward VI should marry the four-year-old Mary, Queen of Scots. The Duke of Somerset, ruler of England during Edward's minority, was determined to teach the Scots a lesson. They were seeking aid from Henry II of France, and Somerset, a man who saw everything in terms of black or white, decided that they must either agree to the wedding and break up their French alliance or he would declare war. The Earl of Arran, who was Regent of

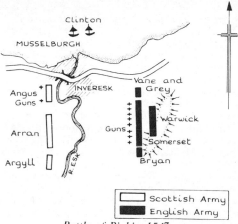

Battle of Pinkie, 1547

Scotland, had a considerable army, some of which had taken part in the siege of St Andrews, which had been held by heretics for over a month and was finally captured in July 1547 with the help of a French fleet.

The English army of nearly eighteen thousand was at Newcastle at the end of August. It was very well organised by Somerset and included fifteen pieces of artillery, two thousand light horse under Sir Francis Bryan, four thousand cavalry under Vane and Grey and six hundred hackbuteers under Sir Peter Mewtus. There was a mounted division similarly equipped under Gamboa, a Spaniard, whose men were the first to use firearms, at the siege of Rhey in 1521. Lord Clinton's fleet accompanied the English army. It consisted of thirty warships and the same number of transports. No army had entered Scotland as well equipped; they even had pioneers to clear the route for their waggons.

Arran, no soldier but a shrewd politician, had arranged his army, which exceeded the English by several thousand — some accounts say it was as many as thirty-four thousand — along the river Esk. The solitary bridge was barricaded and protected by artillery and the sea flank by a raised entrenchment and more artillery. The Earl of Angus with his spearmen formed the left flank, Arran and the men of Stirling, Edinburgh and the Lowlands the centre, and on the right wing were Highlanders under Argyll.

On 9th September the English heavily armed cavalry fought off the Earl of Home's lightly armed horsemen. The next morning Somerset, having refused an offer of single combat from the Scottish Earl of Huntly, decided to put his artillery on Fawside Hill so that it would command the Scottish position. Lord Grey led his cavalry forward, followed by his infantry, and found the Scottish spearmen arranged in squares, the first ranks kneeling, the second sloping forward and the third rank standing. It was like charging a hedgehog and the muddy ground unhorsed many of the cavalry. Grey was wounded and about two hundred of his men were killed. Warwick, in command of the second line, rushed forward with Mewtus's hackbuteers and Gamboa's horsemen. The combined fire and that of the English guns successfully broke the squares and the left wing disintegrated.

Arran, who had held such a fine position, had sacrificed it by trying to cut off the English from their ships. The guns of Clinton's ships in Musselburgh played a decisive part. One lucky shot is supposed to have killed the Master of Graham and twenty-five horsemen. Presumably the Esk was wider and deeper in those days and it is possible that the ships came up the river. The slaughter was frightful; a regiment of monks from Dunfermline was cut down to a man. The Earl of Huntly was captured and Arran retreated to Stirling.

Somerset burnt Leith and after a week retreated to England as his army was short of food. The Scottish alliance with France was strengthened and six thousand French soldiers arrived under Sieur d'Esse, a dashing commander in battle but quarrelsome when not. Mary was sent to France where she married the young Dauphin Francis. In 1550 by the Treaty of Boulogne the English had to give up their French possessions and in Scotland the town of Haddington, fortified by Lord Grey after Pinkie, had already been abandoned because of plague. It was a hollow victory, and the English campaign of 1547 came to be known, by the Scots, as 'the rough wooing'.

Pinkie today

The battlefield of Pinkie is best explored on foot from Inveresk. The ridge held by the English is clearly visible and the actual battle must have covered a large area. It is hard to imagine the English fleet being able to come in close enough to train their cannon on the Scots. Pinkie House in Musselburgh is named after the battle but otherwise has no connection. There is no monument.

LANGSIDE, 13th May 1568
Strathclyde O/S 64 (581 615)

Mary, Queen of Scots, escaped from Lochleven castle at Kinross after being imprisoned there by the Regent Moray (her half-brother) and his confederates. Making for Dumbarton with her supporters, Mary collected a force of five thousand under Argyll and the Hamiltons. Nearly a hundred barons, nine earls, nine

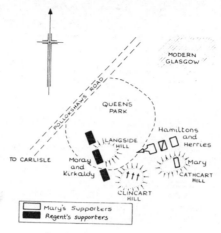

Battle of Langside, 1568

bishops, eighteen lords and twelve abbots and priors signed a pledge to defend Mary and restore her to her rightful throne.

Moray was an astute leader and his smaller force occupied Langside Hill, which is today in Queen's Park, Glasgow. Kirkaldy of Grange commanded two hundred picked musketeers in Langside village. They were mounted behind horsemen for manoeuvrability, and on the left wing Moray's infantry occupied Pathead farm. The Hamiltons attempted to seize the village and Lord Herries led two cavalry charges against Kirkaldy. Moray's cavalry fought them off and the Hamiltons, bypassing Clincart Hill where Moray had stationed his guns, climbed the hill to the village, where they were set on by the musketeers. The spears were levelled and in the cramped site many people were trampled down, especially the Queen's main force, by the fleeing Hamiltons. Kirkaldy now led the reserve down on the flank and front of the Queen's centre and only the cavalry of Lord Herries saved Mary, who had been watching the battle at Cathcart, and enabled her to escape to Dumfries and across the Solway Firth to Workington. Elizabeth took her chance and Mary was never again a free agent. Langside was one of the most decisive battles fought on Scottish soil.

Langside today

The tall granite monument to the battle lies at the south side of Queen's Park, which can be reached from central Glasgow in a few minutes by going south from Central station down Eglinton Street and Pollokshaws Road.

AULDEARN, 9th May 1645

After winning his famous battle at Inverlochy on the slopes of Ben Nevis, Montrose was harried by the two Covenant armies of Baillie and Hurry. He entered Dundee, where his exhausted troops replenished their supplies, and left with the enemy hard on his heels. By devious tracks he reached Speyside and, when he became aware of Hurry's army in front of him he followed it towards Inverness, where there were Covenant reinforcements. Stopping at the little village of Auldearn, Montrose arranged his men during the early hours of 9th May. He placed Macdonald's Irishmen of Antrim, who numbered about five hundred, in a thin line in front of the village, with one wing on the castle hill where the present Boath Doocot stands, and his cavalry of two hundred in two groups were partly hidden by a hill. His own group of eight hundred men was next to the cavalry and a few musketeers held the thin centre where the standard was placed. Hurry had nearly four thousand foot and four hundred cavalry but he could not position them properly because, marching from Nairn, he had spotted the boggy ground, for it had been raining for several days, and as a result his regiments had to deploy. He sent Lawers's men ahead with the Moray Horse under Major Drummond in support

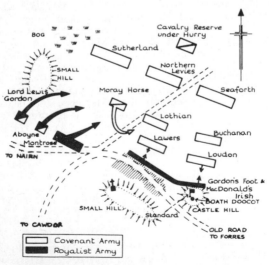

Battle of Auldearn, 1645

on the right. Loudon's regiment advanced on the left and the others followed behind with Hurry taking up the rear with his reserve cavalry.

The Irish, with their backs to stone walls and enclosures, advanced and fought manfully. Gradually, fighting against huge odds, they were forced back. A messenger arrived at Montrose's wing asking for help. 'Will you let the Macdonalds have all the glory of the day?' said Montrose to Lord Gordon, and the two troops of Royalist cavalry, who were hidden from the enemy, charged Hurry's right wing. Major Drummond gave the wrong order in the confusion and the Moray Horse wheeled the wrong way, cutting down some of the Lothian Regiment. Lord Lewis Gordon's horsemen drove the remnants of Drummond's horse off the field but Aboyne wheeled.right and charged the exposed flank of the Lothian and Lawers regiments. Montrose pressed against Buchanan and Loudon. The Irish joined the fight and Hurry, anxious to save his reserves, withdrew to Inverness. Drummond was tried and shot as a traitor in Inverness.

In England, Leven's Scottish army in Yorkshire withdrew to Westmorland to prevent Charles I from linking up with Montrose, and Hurry withdrew to join Baillie. It was not a decisive victory but tactically was probably the most brilliant of all Montrose's victories. About two thousand Covenanters were killed and a few hundred Royalists.

Auldearn today

The Scottish National Trust preserves the Boath Doocot at Auldearn. Nearby, the Trust has erected a viewpoint where there is a plaque with an excellent plan and description of the battle. What is confusing is that the main road between Nairn and Forres (A96) is new and the old road no longer exists. It would seem that if the Macdonalds had posted a man on the castle mound they would have had a commanding view and Montrose must have taken a risk running the battle from the left wing, where it would have been difficult to see exactly what was happening.

ALFORD, 2nd July 1645

Grampian O/S 37 (562 167)

After Auldearn, Montrose turned to meet Baillie, who with an army of about two thousand was over the Dee and blocking the Royalists' route to the south. Baillie had lost some of his best men to another Covenanter, Lindsay, who was raising a new army in Perth. Montrose, after resting his troops in Elgin, lost the Gordons, who went home to Strathbogie, where their land was threatened by Baillie's men. Montrose retired after threatening

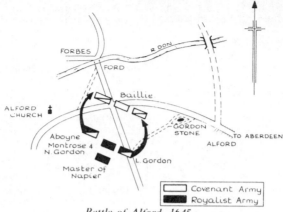

Battle of Alford, 1645

Lindsay and waited for reinforcements to arrive. He took up a strong position at Corgaff castle on the Don. The Gordons returned under Lord Gordon when Montrose had moved to Pitlarg Castle near the Gordon seat of Huntly. Baillie was a few miles north at Keith and, having discovered that some of Montrose's Irish were absent recruiting, decided to attack. Moving south again, Montrose took up a commanding position on Gallows Hill near the village of Alford. With a bog protecting his rear, Montrose calculated that Baillie would cross the Don at the ford of Boat of Forbes nearby.

Montrose placed the Gordons on his right and Aboyne's horse on his left, with the Highlanders in the centre and a small reserve under the Master of Napier behind. Baillie crossed the ford, led on by the impetuous Balcarres, an experienced cavalry commander whose horse outnumbered Montrose's horse by nearly two to one. Infuriated by seeing so much of his family's cattle in the rear of Baillie's army, young Lord Gordon led his right wing forward immediately. Balcarres's line broke but reformed and a cavalry battle ensued which was joined by Nathaniel Gordon's foot, who threw down their muskets and hacked at the enemy's horses with their swords. Aboyne led his horse round the opposing wing, which fled leaving the Covenanters' centre pressed on all sides. Most fought where they stood and Balcarres and Baillie escaped with a few survivors.

Lord Gordon charged the retreating cavalry once too often and was shot from behind. The battle was a clear victory for Montrose but he lost his friend and gallant cavalry commander. With the exception of Lindsay's raw army there was no one left for Montrose to conquer in Scotland and yet Naseby had been fought in June and the King's army in the south had dwindled, while that of Cromwell was only just beginning to recognise its new leader.

Alford today

Alford village, which is twenty-five miles west of Aberdeen on A944, is modern and the site of the battle is the crossroads on the other side of the village. The river was much wider in those days and Gallows Hill is the height above the crossroads. A new road leads to the Gordon stone, which is railed off at the edge of a field and looks as if it has been there much longer than the battle date. The Ordnance Survey crossed swords sign is not on the generally agreed site of the battle.

KILSYTH, 15th August 1645
Strathclyde O/S 64 (741 787)

Auldearn and Alford saw the supremacy of Montrose's small army in the Highlands but the south of Scotland still had to be captured from the hands of the Covenanters. In July Baillie resigned from the Committee but was ordered to regain command of the new army which assembled at Perth on 24th July.

Montrose was strengthened by the return of Macdonald with fourteen hundred Irish and West Highlanders and Patrick Graham arrived with the men of Atholl. He was now strong enough to threaten Perth but without cavalry he could not do more than this. Aboyne had been sent out again for further mounted reinforcements, having failed to produce any the first time. Eventually he arrived with two hundred Gordon cavalry and some mounted musketeers.

Baillie caught some of the hangers-on of Montrose's army in Methven wood near Perth and slaughtered them. His forces now numbered six thousand foot and eight hundred horse to Montrose's four thousand five hundred foot and five hundred horse. On 10th August Montrose went to Kinross and then turned on Castle Campbell at Dollar which he burned. He then crossed the Forth at the Ford of Frew to get between Baillie, who had collected his Fife levies, and the new recruits from Glasgow under the Earl of Lanark. He found a commanding position at Kilsyth where he waited for Baillie's army to catch up.

Baillie was hampered by his Committee which had different views on how to fight Montrose. When a flank march to get round Montrose's army to the heights above him was proposed he was powerless to stop it. Some Covenanters under Major Haldane saw a few cottages occupied by the Macleans and, breaking their positions, they rushed on them. Macdonald, seeing the Macleans in action, broke out of line, charged the enemy and with the

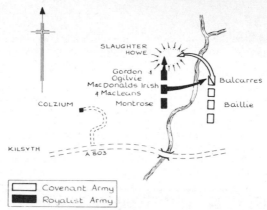

Battle of Kilsyth, 1645

Macleans cut the Covenanters into two groups. The Gordon cavalry under Aboyne and his brother went to the height threatened by Baillie's horse and when Aboyne was hard pressed the Ogilvies, commanded by their sixty-year-old chief, charged Balcarres just as he was about to take the hill.

Baillie still had his Fife reserve and tried to rush them up to the rescue of his fast dwindling army. They were not expert soldiers and many had fought at Tippermuir the year before when they had seen Montrose's army at its fiercest. They turned and fled.

The Fife men were cut down in their hundreds, for the Highlanders were out to revenge the slaughter of their women-folk in Methven wood. Barely one hundred of the foot escaped. The cavalry were more fortunate and some escaped by ship to Berwick; others went to Stirling or Carlisle.

Kilsyth today

The battlefield of Kilsyth is mostly covered by a reservoir. The nearby topography is or was called by bloodthirsty names like Slaughter Howe, Drum Burn, Kill-the-many Butts. There are a few relics at the manor of Colzium which is off the A803 a few miles before Kilsyth when coming from Stirling. In the Argyll and Sutherland Highlanders Regimental Museum in Stirling Castle is a silver relief of the battle on a statue of Montrose on horseback.

PHILIPHAUGH, 13th September 1645
Borders O/S 73 (445 282)

After Kilsyth Montrose occupied Glasgow but instead of gaining support his army disintegrated. Macdonald and half the

Irish troops left for Galloway and Lord Aboyne returned to the north with the Gordons. With scarcely seven hundred men Montrose set out for the borders, as instructed by Charles I, hoping to pick up recruits on the way, especially from the Earls of Home and Roxburgh. But he was to be disappointed, and in England General Leslie, who had been besieging Hereford, moved north with about six thousand men, most of whom were mounted.

Advised by Lord Erskine to retreat, Montrose was determined to find allies, but on reaching Kelso no one came forward and at Jedburgh the local laird was a Covenanter general. On 12th September the small Royalist force reached the junction of the Yarrow and Ettrick rivers. He camped here with the rivers protecting two flanks, a steep hill to the north and only the track from Selkirk providing any easy access. During the night Lord Linton, the son of the Earl of Traquair, withdrew and according to tradition went to Leslie in his camp, which was between Galashiels and Selkirk, probably at Sunderland Hall, where he drove out some Royalists.

Early next morning Leslie was on the move. He divided his army into two groups, one of which consisted of two thousand dragoons and was commanded by Agnew of Lochnaw. Guided by a local man, they went round Linglie Hill and advanced on Montrose's rear. The other under Leslie moved down the riverbank towards Philiphaugh. It was a misty day and Montrose with a few horsemen was at a house in West Port in Selkirk when he was roused by his scoutmaster who told him the news. The sudden emergence from the mist of Leslie's cavalry on the Irish was a shock. They had built some shallow trenches but Douglas's men fled at once, and the Irish were soon hopelessly outnumbered when Agnew's men burst down on their rear.

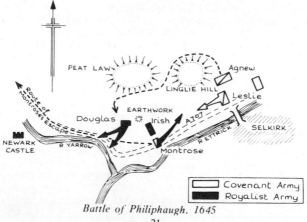

Battle of Philiphaugh. 1645

21

Montrose, collecting a small force of cavalry, crossed the Ettrick, joined his army, which was already under attack, and attempted to hold up Leslie's horse. His few cavalry fought bravely but soon realising that all was lost they fled over Minch Moor to Traquair House, where they were refused admission. The Irish under their adjutant Stewart surrendered and were slaughtered on their march to captivity, along with their womenfolk, who were mostly shot in the courtyard of nearby Newark Castle. Montrose and about thirty followers reached the safety of the Highlands but the year of victories was over.

Philiphaugh today

The battlefield stands in private land in the grounds of Philiphaugh House, just off the A708 about two miles west of Selkirk. There is an ivy-covered monument to the memory of 'the Covenanters who fought and gained the battle' next to the tennis court. The field opposite is called Battlefield and there are traces of an earthwork at one end. Permission should be obtained to see the monument.

DUNBAR, 3rd September 1650

Lothian O/S 67 (702 768)

After the execution of King Charles I, his son was proclaimed king in Scotland (the Covenanters forced him to sign their document upholding Presbyterianism). The Marquis of Argyll, who a few months before had executed the unfortunate Montrose after his defeat at Carbisdale, set about building an army to conquer the English forces under Cromwell. With David Leslie, Cromwell's former ally at Marston Moor, as its leader, the Scottish army consisted of 'minister's sons, clerks and such as who hardly ever saw or heard of any sword but that of the spirit'.

With the navy to support him, Cromwell moved up towards Edinburgh where Leslie checked him by constructing entrenchments from Holyrood to Leith. In August 1650 Cromwell, based at Dunbar where he was supported by his fleet, tried again to outflank Leslie. The latter stripped the surrounding country of all provisions and surrounded Dunbar, putting his main force on Doon Hill where it could watch the enemy and block the escape route at Cockburnspath and Ewieside Hill. Writing to Haselrig, who was with the reinforcements at Newcastle, Cromwell remarked: 'we are upon an engagement very difficult'. With disease in his army, Cromwell knew he must attack. Leslie withdrew on 2nd September and lined his army up on the Spott burn near Broxburn.

Setting out before dawn on the 3rd, six cavalry regiments,

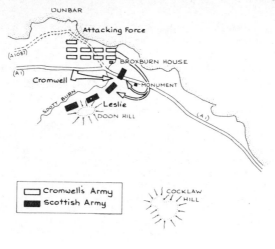

Battle of Dunbar, 1650

commanded by Fleetwood, Whalley and Lambert, with Monck's three infantry regiments attacked the Scots over the burn. The Scots had extinguished the match used to light their muskets owing to the night rain. They put up a stiff resistance in spite of this, but Cromwell's own regiment 'did come seasonably in and at push of pike did repel the stoutest regiment the enemy had there'. The second cavalry charge 'made the Lord of Hosts as stubble to our swords'. Forcing their way through the gap by the sea, the English turned and caught Leslie's main force in the rear. Nearly three thousand were killed or wounded and twice that number captured.

Edinburgh fell to the victorious Cromwell and Leslie withdrew to Stirling. The religious leaders said that the defeat was due to the estrangement of the Lord from an army which fought for an unconverted king. Leslie's final thrust the following year at Worcester also failed. That battle was fought on the anniversary of Dunbar and the Scots are a superstitious race.

Dunbar today

The battle site is beside the A1 where a monument stands next to a bus shelter and the Portland cement works. It is easy to pass by without noticing the words of Thomas Carlyle: 'Here took place the brunt or essential agony of the battle of Dunbar'. Carved on the pedestal are 'The Covenant' and 'The Lord of Hosts', representing the two beliefs that the armies fought for. As battle

23

monuments go it is one of the finest. As battle sites go it is ruined by the cement works, main road and bus shelter.

BOTHWELL BRIDGE, 22nd June 1679
Strathclyde O/S 64 (711 578)

Charles II restored the bishops to Scotland and episcopacy replaced Presbyterianism as the official religion. The Duke of Lauderdale enforced the law and all prayer meetings of the Covenanters had to be held outside, with sentries posted to give warnings in the event of the arrival of royal troops.

At Drumclog near Strathaven in June 1679 the Life Guards under Viscount Dundee were outnumbered in a bog by the Covenanters led by Robert Hamilton, Balfour of Burleigh and Hackston of Rathillet. Thirty-eight were killed and Dundee only escaped in the nick of time, with his horse mortally wounded. Charles II, on hearing of the disaster, put the Scottish loyalists under the command of the Duke of Monmouth, who had recently seen service in Holland, and with only four troops of cavalry Monmouth joined Dundee in Falkirk. The Earl of Linlithgow was in command of the foot, many of which were militia, and on 22nd June Monmouth reached Bothwell on the road to Hamilton, where the rebels, commanded by their preachers, had defended the bridge, which was 120 feet long and had a central fortified gateway and paving of stones from the Clyde beneath.

The Macfarlanes charged the bridge which was held by Rathillet's marksmen. The ammunition of the defenders soon ran out. They fell back and the Lennox Highlanders crossed the bridge followed by Dundee and the cavalry, which soon put the rebels to flight, extracting cruel revenge for their fellow soldiers killed at Drumclog. The Covenanters fled to Hamilton, which was partially defended by Balfour of Burleigh and their two thousand horse commanded by Robert Hamilton. Russell and Barscobe went to Cumloch, and thence a few escaped to Holland.

Thirteen hundred prisoners were taken and shut up in Greyfriars churchyard at Edinburgh. Most were freed when they signed a bond giving up the Covenant. Those that refused were shipped to the colonies. Two hundred were drowned off Orkney and others died in the dreadful conditions at Leith prior to their departure.

The Duke of Monmouth took pity on the Covenanters and tried to prevent any recriminations, but shortly after this he fell out of favour. The bravery of the defenders of the bridge was not lost on him however and six years later similar untrained peasants formed his army at Sedgemoor.

1. The Wallace Monument and old bridge at Stirling. This bridge is about a mile downstream from the site of the bridge where Sir William Wallace resoundingly defeated the English in 1297.

2. The battlefield of Bannockburn was the scene of Robert Bruce's great victory in 1314, establishing Scottish independence from England.

3. The bronze statue of Bruce at Bannockburn marks his position at the start of the battle. The work of C. d'O. Pilkington Jackson, the 3½-ton statue was unveiled by the Queen in 1964.

4. Auldearn (9th May 1645) was one of Montrose's most brilliant victories over the Covenanters. The Boath Doocot, preserved by the National Trust for Scotland, stands on the hill where he positioned some of his troops.

5. In the courtyard of Newark Castle near Selkirk the womenfolk of Montrose's Irish troops were slaughtered after the battle of Philiphaugh (13th September 1645), when the Covenanters under Leslie defeated Montrose, to end his year of victories.

6. At the pass of Killiecrankie on 27th July 1689 the Jacobite army under Dundee awaited Mackay's Government army. The Jacobites won the day, but Mackay eventually went on to subdue the Highlands.

7. The monument that marks the mound where the officers of both sides killed in the battle of Killiecrankie are buried also commemorates a young officer killed in Malaya in 1950.

8. In 1719 Jacobite supporters made another attempt to secure the throne for the Old Pretender. But despite the assistance of three hundred Spanish troops, the small Highland army was defeated by General Wightman in Glen Shiel on 10th June.

9. *The cairn commemorating the battle of Culloden on 16th April 1746, when the Duke of Cumberland crushed Bonnie Prince Charlie's Highlanders, ending Jacobite hopes once and for all.*

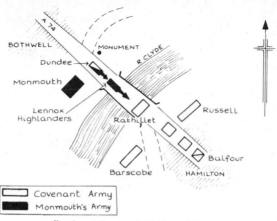

Battle of Bothwell Bridge, 1679

Bothwell Bridge today

The battlefield can be visited on the A47 between Glasgow and Hamilton. The modern bridge has a monument on the Bothwell bank which was erected at the beginning of this century. Parking is very difficult and it is probably easier to leave your car in Bothwell and walk from there. Monmouth is supposed to have occupied the highest point above the bridge.

KILLIECRANKIE, 27th July 1689
Tayside O/S 43 (905 639)

The opposition to the revolution in 1688 was negligible in England but in Scotland James VII's lieutenant was Viscount Dundee, an energetic and loyal soldier who had been Monmouth's second in command at Bothwell Bridge. Supported by the loyal Highland clans, Dundee made his base at Blair Atholl, where the Marquis was sitting on the fence, waiting to see who would win the forthcoming encounter, for the Scottish Convention had on William's orders sent General Mackay and a strong body of regular troops to attack and defeat Dundee.

Arranging his army on the slopes of the hill behind and above Urrard House, Dundee waited for Mackay's soldiers to come out of Killiecrankie pass on their way to Blair Castle. His men were not hidden and Mackay must have realised that, although Dundee had a commanding position, his own forces were superior and his two troops of horse, placed in the centre, had some room to manoeuvre, while Dundee's few horsemen had a perilous hill to descend before they could come into action. Mackay's force numbered four thousand four hundred to Dundee's two thousand four hundred.

Dundee arranged the Macleans on his right wing, then three hundred Irish under Cannon, then Clanranald's Macdonalds. On his left wing were the Macdonalds of Sleat, then a mixed group of clans mostly Macleans, then Lochiel's Camerons, some of whom were sent down to occupy a cottage just above Urrard House. The few horse were commanded by Sir William Wallace, and Dundee, conspicuous in a silver and buff coat with a green scarf, placed himself in the centre, the standard of King James VII carried by Macdonell of Glengarry.

For two hours the two armies faced each other, Dundee waiting for the sun to move round until it was shining in the faces of his enemy. Mackay's three guns were firing but seem to have done little damage. At half past seven in the evening Dundee gave the signal to charge and, standing in his saddle to encourage his cavalry, was struck down in the opening minutes of the battle.

The Highlanders rushed forward firing their muskets when within range, then discarding them and rushing on with dirks and claymores. The enemy reeled and gave way. Belhaven's and Annandale's cavalry, attacked by sixteen horsemen under the Earl of Dunfermline, retreated in disorder and only Leven's regiment and part of that of Hastings remained on the scene with Mackay. Their accurate fire kept the clans at bay while they retreated, pursued by some of Wallace's horsemen who had made a different descent from the hill to that made by Dunfermline.

Four hundred men including Mackay finally reached Stirling castle. Dundee's body was taken to Old Blair where it lies buried in the churchyard. Some thousand of Mackay's men were killed and five hundred taken prisoner. Two hundred Highlanders were killed by accurate infantry musketry, including Dundee. Colonel Cannon took over the army but failed to capture Dunkeld, which was stoutly held by Clelland's Cameronian regiment. The Jacobite victory of Dundee at Killiecrankie was an isolated incident and one which did not stop Mackay from eventually subduing the Highlands.

Killiecrankie today.

The Scottish National Trust in 1964 erected a small museum which is now a visitors' centre with information about the battle. This, with a large car park, stands on the A9 north of Pitlochry. The battle site however is further north on the lane leading to Orchilmore. The mound where the officers of both sides were buried is surmounted by a monument erected in 1950 to the memory of Ian Campbell Younger of Urrard, killed in Malaya at the age of twenty-four. It is a haunting spot and the boggy

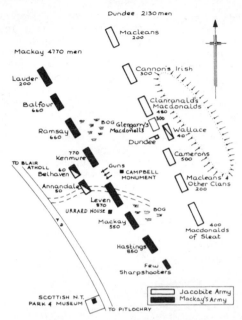

Battle of Killiecrankie, 1689

ground and trees, assuming they were there in 1689, would have made cavalry action very difficult, which may explain why sixteen Jacobite horse made such an impression on Mackay's hundred and ten. There is a monument to Dundee in the ruined church at Old Blair.

SHERIFFMUIR, 13th November 1715
Central O/S 57 (822 017)

On 6th September 1715 the Jacobite standard of James VIII was raised at Braemar by the Earl of Mar, who had been dismissed by George I from his post as Secretary of State for Scotland. With a commission from James VIII and the promise of help from France the 1715 rebellion started with far more chance of success than its successor thirty years later. The Protestant loyalists rallied at Stirling, the local militias under the command of General Wightman and under overall command of the Duke of Argyll, a capable soldier and statesman.

Mar dallied at Perth while the clans came in slowly. On 10th November he left with nearly ten thousand men and joined General Gordon at Auchterarder. Plans were made to approach the Forth in four divisions and to avoid Stirling where Argyll's force numbered only three thousand men. Argyll's spies brought word that Gordon's men were approaching Dunblane and on Sunday 12th November he moved first, occupied the town and camped his army two miles north-east above Kippenross House. He knew the area well as the local militia used Sheriffmuir as a training ground.

Mar was annoyed that Gordon had been unable to take Dunblane and on the approach of darkness he ordered his men to camp at Kinbuck. 'It cannot be said we had a front or rear any more than has a barrel of herrings' was the comment of the Master of Sinclair. Early next morning Mar drew up his forces (see plan) at the eastern end of Sherrifmuir, his left wing protected by a bog. Argyll drew up his army, which though small in number was superior in cavalry. The burns had frozen over in the night, so he had chosen his position from a cavalry commander's point of view. Argyll scouted out the Jacobites' position from his right wing (he stood where the Gathering Stone can still be seen) and ordered his drums to beat the advance.

When the two armies came in sight of each other, both right wings of their front ranks outflanked the opposition. Mar quickly ordered the Macleans to charge; the Duke of Argyll, spotting the Jacobite left wing out of line as it circled a bog, brought up his heavy cavalry and only a gallant stand by the Fife and Angus horse prevented the complete collapse of Mar's left wing. Meanwhile the Royalist left wing collapsed and General Whitham fled back to Stirling. From Argyll's right the Scots Greys and Evans's Dragoons slaughtered the light horsemen opposite them while the Macraes in Seaforth's battalions were killed almost to a man.

When Argyll returned with about one thousand men he found that he was outnumbered, so he ordered Wightman to take up a defensive position with his cannon. Seeing what had happened to his other wing, the Earl of Mar retreated, losing four cannon, thirteen colours and nearly eight hundred killed or captured. On the other hand he had captured four colours and fourteen hundred arms; Argyll had lost two hundred and ninety killed and over a hundred taken prisoner.

The rising soon collapsed, partly due to the capture by Argyll of so many Highland leaders and the desertion of the clans at Perth. When James finally arrived it was too late actually to raise an army again. Mar fled to France, where he died in 1732.

The surprising feature of the battle is the behaviour of both commanders in charging with their wings and ignoring the rest of their armies. Mar did send a messenger to General Hamilton, who

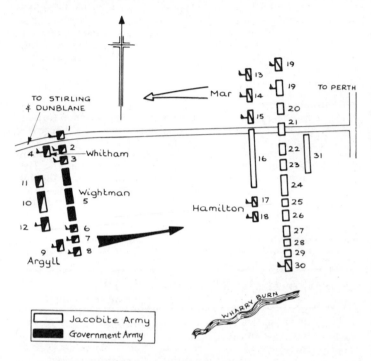

Battle of Sheriffmuir, 1715

GOVERNMENT ARMY (ARGYLL)

Front Line: *1 Carpenter's Dragoons; 2 Kerr's Dragoons; 3, 4 Stair's Dragoons; 5 Six battalions (1,800 men) under General Wightman; 6 Stair's Dragoons; 7 Scots Greys; 8 Evans's Dragoons; 9 Sixty volunteer gentlemen.*
Second Line: *10 Two battalions of infantry; 11, 12 Dragoons.*

JACOBITE ARMY (MAR)

Front Line: *13, 14 Huntly's Horse; 15 Stirling Horse; 16 General Gordon's Highlanders (ten battalions); 17 Perth Horse; 18 Fife Horse.*
Second line: *19 Earl Marischal's Horse (two battalions); 20, 21, 22 Seaforth's Highlanders (three battalions); 23, 24 Huntly's Highlanders (two battalions); 25 Panmure; 26 Tullibardine; 27 Drummond; 28 Strathallan; 29 Robertsons; 30 Angus Horse; 31 Reserve (800 men).*

commanded his left, but according to one account the messenger was a traitor and delayed his message until it was too late. The ground is hilly in the middle, like a large-scale camber, and it is possible that Argyll only saw the wing he attacked, but this does not explain the conduct of his centre troops. Mar's centre fought with his right and in both armies artillery appears to have played no part.

Sheriffmuir today

The battlefield is easily found by taking the right-hand turning on the A9 just after the road up to Stirling University. There is a large monument to the Macraes and behind this, 450 yards along the footpath, the small gathering stone can be seen by a clump of firs. It is covered by iron hoops to deter souvenir hunters. The Macrae monument reads: 'In memory of the Macraes killed at Sheriffmuir 13 Nov. 1715 when defending the Royal House of Stuart. The Kintail and Lochalsh companies formed part of the left wing of the army and fell almost to a man.' In the Clan Donnachie Museum near Blair Atholl the Robertsons' famous crystal stone, known as the *Clach na Brattich,* which was carried in the battle and at Culloden, can be seen.

GLEN SHIEL, 10th June 1719
Highland O/S 33 (991 133)

The 1715 rising cost the Jacobite cause nearly £12,000,000 and by 1718 the supporters of the Old Pretender had run out of money as the French pension paid to Mary of Modena, who died in May, was lost. The one hope of the Jacobites was Cardinal Alberoni of Spain, who was prompted by the Duke of Ormonde to raise a fleet and an invading armada to invade England. By early March 1719 it set sail with twenty-nine ships and five thousand troops. The same misfortune hit this armada as its more famous predecessor — storm. The ships were scattered and most returned home to Cadiz. However, two frigates with three hundred Spanish troops under Keith, Earl Marischal, left San Sebastian on 8th March and reached Lewis in April. They were joined by the Earl of Seaforth and the Marquis of Tullibardine. After argument over who was in command, Tullibardine organised the setting up of an arsenal in Eilean Donan castle in Loch Duich. Keith sent the Spanish ships home and it was not long before three English frigates appeared, the *Worcester* under Captain Boyle, the *Enterprize* under Captain Herdman and the *Flamborough* under Captain Heldersley, and opened fire on the castle.

The Spaniards escaped with some of the arms and, joining Rob Roy's forces with about fifteen hundred Highlanders, mostly

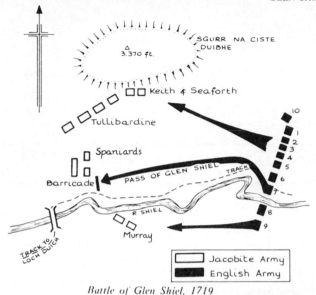

Battle of Glen Shiel, 1719

1, 2, 3 Grenadiers; 4 Montagu; 5 Harrison; 6 Huffel's Dutch; 7 Robertson's Dragoons and four Cohorn mortars; 8 Clayton's under Colonel Reading; 9 Monro Highlanders; 10 Sutherland.

Mackenzies, Macraes and Macgregors, who came in, they proceeded to march round the Loch and into the pass of Glen Shiel where Seaforth, the Spaniards and Tullibardine took up a defensive position guarding the bridge.

General Wightman (see Sheriffmuir) was dispatched with about eleven hundred men, including a Dutch regiment and four Cohorn mortars, to put down the rising. He drew up his men at Glen Shiel facing the bridge on 10th June. At about 5 p.m. his mortars opened fire and his regiment on the right wing found their way round the back of the Highlanders' line and routed them. The Spaniards were made of sterner stuff and retired to another defensive position, finally agreeing to surrender the following day. About twenty-one of Wightman's men were killed and a hundred and twenty-one wounded. On the Jacobite side the losses were only ten killed. Earl Keith was badly wounded but managed to escape and find his way to the Continent. Seaforth was wounded by a grenade — Glen Shiel is one of the earliest examples of grenadiers in action — but he and Tullibardine also made their escape. Thus ended the Nineteen.

Glen Shiel today

The site of the battle is about half a mile east of the new bridge and the grave of one of Montagu's officers is visible near a waterfall. Bullets are still occasionally found in the river bed. Eilean Donan castle, which was blown up by the *Worcester,* was restored by Colonel Macrae-Gilstrap in the 1920s. The Spaniards supposedly threw their treasure into a deep lochan nearby before they surrendered, but this is more legend than fact. The castle is open to the public.

PRESTONPANS, 21st September 1745
Lothian O/S 66 (402 742)

Prince Charles Edward Stuart landed on the west coast of Scotland in July 1745, accompanied by nine men and a few arms. England was at war with France and the planned French invasion of 1744 had been destroyed by a gale. The Scots were armed with broad sword, dirk and targe (a small circular shield) and some had pistols. Very few had 'muskets, fuses or fowling pieces'. They were fast moving and fierce when they charged. The English redcoats had muskets with bayonets. These needed ramrods for loading and the cartridge had to be bitten to sprinkle powder into the firing pan so that they were too slow to reload at Prestonpans, and the weather was against them at Falkirk, where the Scottish army, although exhausted by its long march to Derby and back, defeated Hawley's dragoons and infantry in the fog and rain. It was only at Culloden that the English infantrymen, firing in three ranks, one rank at a time and then thrusting their bayonets at the unguarded side of the Highlanders, were effective.

Prince Charles's Highland army marched into Edinburgh at noon on 17th September 1745, having captured it during the night without any resistance. Only the castle remained in Government hands. Near Dunbar, however, was Sir John Cope with six squadrons of dragoons, three companies of foot and some Scottish volunteers. The Highlanders had few arms and no mobile artillery; their cavalry was about forty men and their main force numbered two thousand four hundred. Cope's army numbered three thousand and included artillery manned by naval gunners.

On 19th September Prince Charles held a council of war at Duddingston where his Highlanders were camping. Next day they moved out towards Musselburgh. Cope moved more slowly to Haddington and took up a position on the 20th near Preston House, less than a mile from the sea, with a cornfield in which his dragoons could manoeuvre and the marshy Tranent meadows protecting his south flank. Lord George Murray, in command of the Highland vanguard, immediately positioned the Prince's army

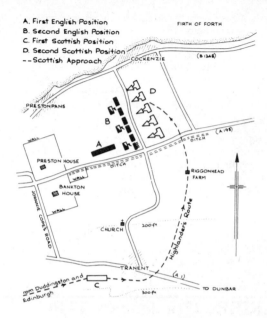

A. First English Position
B. Second English Position
C. First Scottish Position
D. Second Scottish Position
-- Scottish Approach

Battle of Prestonpans, 1745

on Falside Hill near Tranent, where he could observe the Government army without difficulty.

The strength of Cope's position was soon apparent to Lord George, who realised that the Tranent meadows were poor ground for charging Highlanders, for as well as being very marshy in places they were crossed by dry stone dykes. A local man, Anderson, suggested a hidden path to the west of Rigganhead farm that would bring the Highland army round to Cope's weakest flank, the east. Setting off at 4 a.m. on Saturday 21st September, they had reached the farm when a shot rang out. One of Cope's patrols had spotted them. The Government army was hastily repositioned facing east with the guns on the right wing and three dragoon squadrons in the second line. Next to the guns were Colonel Gardiner's dragoons. The Colonel, no longer a fit man, had played a large part in the victory at Preston over the Jacobites in 1715.

The Camerons on the Highland left charged as soon as the last of the rearguard had arrived on the field. With few shots from their guns and mortars taking effect, the Government gunners fled, the dragoons and artillery regiment following them. With the sun in their eyes and the long line of advancing Highlanders in front, the Government army thought they were outnumbered. The dragoons on the left wing rode off towards Prestonpans and Cope himself, having tried to rally his men, led a party of four hundred stragglers up a side road (now known as Johnnie Cope's road) to the Highland first position. They did not stop until they reached the safety of Berwick-upon-Tweed. Colonel Gardiner, whose home, Bankton House (see map) was beside the battlefield, was mortally wounded by an axe and died the following day in the manse at Tranent. He was buried in Tranent churchyard. Some five hundred Government infantry and dragoons were killed, fourteen hundred captured and many wounded. The Highlanders lost thirty killed and seventy wounded and on their march into England that followed, the ballad 'Hey Johnnie Cope are ye walking yet?' was sung by the conquerors as a marching song.

Prestonpans today

Take the A1 from Edinburgh to Tranent, where turn left to Cockenzie past the church to a railway bridge and the junction with A198. The area through which the Highlanders marched is now an open-cast coal mine.

FALKIRK, 17th January 1746
Central O/S 65 (875 790)

The retreat of the Jacobites from Derby did not mean the immediate end of the Forty-five. Edinburgh was back in Government hands and so too was Stirling castle, but Perth was the rallying point of Jacobite reinforcements, some of whom had sailed from France into Montrose unopposed. In January 1746 Prince Charles's army besieged Stirling castle. In Edinburgh General Hawley took command of the infantry and dragoons, of which there were twelve regiments, nine having recently landed from Flanders. Hawley's one weakness was artillery. He had a motley collection of guns from Edinburgh castle commanded by Captain Cunningham, who had to raise a scratch force of gunners from country people.

By 16th January Hawley's army had camped at Falkirk. In numbers it was about eight thousand men and the General's aide-de-camp, Stuart Mackenzie, has left us a graphic picture of the ensuing battle in a letter to Robert Trevor, which is preserved in the Trevor papers in the Buckinghamshire County Record Office.

Murray had originally sent out Lord Elcho's cavalry to reconnoitre near Linlithgow where he hoped to seize some stores.

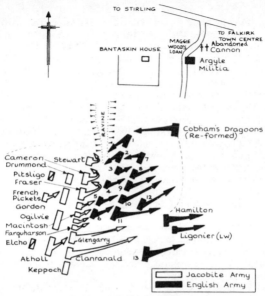

Battle of Falkirk, 1746

ENGLISH ARMY
1 Ligonier (RW); 2 Price; 3 Royals; 4 Pulteney; 5 Cholmondeley; 6 Wolfe; 7 Barrel; 8 Battereau; 9 Fleming; 10 Munro; 11 Blakeney; 12 Howard; 13 Glasgow Volunteers.

JACOBITE ARMY
The Macintosh company fought side by side with the Macphersons (left) and the Mackenzies (right).

He was informed of Hawley's approach and on 15th January the Highlanders, about nine thousand in number now that the Perth reinforcements had come in, drew up in battle order on Plean Muir two miles south-east of Bannockburn. Murray saw the advantage of occupying the hill above Falkirk and sent his infantry there in two columns, the horse under Lord John Drummond taking the main road from Stirling, where the Duke of Perth was left with one thousand men in the castle siege lines. On 17th January, while the Jacobites were on the move, Hawley was being entertained to breakfast at Callander House by the Countess of Kilmarnock. It was not until the afternoon that he realised the seriousness of the situation and ordered his army forward through the narrow Maggie Wood's Loan on to the hill.

Cunningham's cannon stuck in a bog on their way up the hill and played no part in the engagement. The Jacobites were in three lines with the Macdonalds on the right, the Stewarts on the left and a deep ravine in front of their left. The right wing was protected by a bog. The Government troops were in two lines with the Argyll Militia in reserve. In the centre were Hamilton and Wolfe's regiments and the driving rain and poor visibility did not encourage the men of Ligonier's dragoons who were given the order to charge. Murray commanded the Jacobite right and gave the order to fire when the dragoons were a few yards off. The result was devastating, and Clanranald's men dashed into the fray. Hamilton's dragoons turned and fled, cutting a path through the newly raised Glasgow Volunteers. 'What hindered the rebels from pursuing our left, God knows', wrote Mackenzie. Not one in twenty muskets would work due to the rain and the Jacobites, who were more accustomed to using swords than muskets, charged across the ravine.

Unfortunately for them there was no commander of their left wing and the three regiments of Price, Stanhope and Barrel stood firm and caught them in the flank. Cobham's men reformed and came back up the hill but Murray had brought forward the Atholl regiment who drove them off. Hawley was now off the field and three pieces of Cunningham's artillery were salvaged, the rest falling into Jacobite hands.

'If the victory was to be given to either side', wrote Mackenzie, 'it certainly was theirs rather than ours; our loss and theirs I believe are pretty near equal.'

The surprising result of Falkirk was the retreat of the Highlanders. Instead of assuming a defensive position at Falkirk they renewed the siege of Stirling castle without success and retreated to Perth and Inverness. Cumberland took over command of the Government army and Culloden was not far away. Lord George Murray realised that the winter was unsuitable for keeping an army in the field and they would do better in the spring. The deserters worried Murray but Charles was anxious to hold his ground and to wait for further French reinforcements. It was Murray who had his way, so that Falkirk was merely a temporary halt to the Government army. The man who laughed loudest at Hawley's defeat was Cope, who was £10,000 the richer after winning a bet that Hawley would meet the same fate that Cope himself had met much earlier at Prestonpans.

Falkirk today

The town of Falkirk is so industrialised that most of the battlefield has now been built on. However Maggie Wood's Loan can easily be found on the Stirling road and there is a battle monument nearby erected in 1927. General Hawley's home, West Green House, at Hartley Wintney in Hampshire belongs to the National Trust and contains a few relics of the battle.

CULLODEN, 16th April 1746

Highland O/S 27 (736 452)

The Jacobite victory at Falkirk over Hawley's dragoons and foot was a 'scrambling floundering affair' and the arrival of the Duke of Cumberland in place of the luckless Hawley forced Charles Stuart to withdraw to Perth, where the heavy guns were abandoned. He took up quarters in Inverness. The Government post at Fort Augustus was captured and the post at Fort William was besieged. A detachment of Highlanders was sent north to rescue the gold and supplies from France, which had been landed on the north coast but had been seized by Government troops.

Cumberland's army arrived at Nairn on 14th April. It numbered nearly ten thousand and his artillery consisted of ten three-pounders and six mortars. The Jacobites were suffering from lack of food and from desertion. Charles's army numbered about four thousand nine hundred, with thirteen guns of different sizes and a mixture of ammunition. On the night of the 15th April the Highlanders attempted a night attack on Cumberland's camp, but two miles short of the camp a drum sounded and they had to retreat. Had this attack succeeded, Culloden would never have been fought.

The open moor at Drummossie had been chosen by O'Sullivan, the Prince's Quartermaster-General. It was totally unsuited to the Highland method of attack. Each flank was protected by a drystone wall which would enable the enemy cavalry to dash round the wings without being seen. Murray had arranged with the Macdonalds that his Atholl men should have the right flank position in a rota system and the former were upset by the loss of face on the left wing. The battle started with a cannonade that lasted fifteen minutes. Why Charles's officers let their men face such devastating fire is difficult to understand. The Jacobite guns did little damage, except for one that arrived late and was positioned in the south-west corner of the walled enclosure. The right wing could wait no longer and Murray urged them forward. The two Hanoverian regiments facing them, Barrel's and Munro's, were soon in the thick of it. Their officers had trained them to attack the man on their right so that they could pierce his unprotected side.

The Highlanders were so bunched up that only a few could fire. The same thing was happening in the centre. 'No one that attacked us escaped alive for we gave no quarter nor would accept of any,' said an officer in Munro's regiment. The Macdonalds retreated on the left and Keppoch, their leader, charged with a small handful, only to be shot down. Cumberland now ordered up

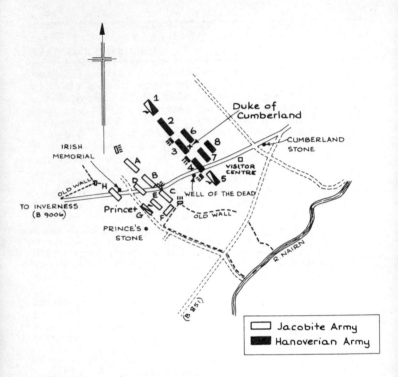

Battle of Culloden, 1746

JACOBITE ARMY
A Macdonalds and Duke of Perth; B Farquharsons, Macleans, Macintoshes, Frasers, Stewarts of Appin, Camerons; C Lord George Murray's Atholl Brigade; D Irish under Brigadier Stapleton; E Lord Drummond's Royal Scots, Lord Lewis Gordon; F Ogilvy Regiment; G Fitzjames Horse and Life Guards; H Reserve under Lord Balmerino.

HANOVERIAN ARMY
1 Cobham's Dragoons, Kingston's Horse; 2 Pulteney, Royal Scots; 3 Cholmondeley, Price, Royal Scots Fusiliers; 4 Munro, Barrel; 5 Wolfe; 6 Battereau, Howard, Fleming; 7 Bligh, Sempill, Ligonier; 8 Blakeney.

The Duke of Cumberland is positioned in front of Howard's Regiment, and the Prince behind the Fitzjames Horse.

his horse and only the steadiness of the Irish troops in the second line and the solitary gun in the park prevented a complete massacre on the left wing. On the right the small band of horse under Lord Elcho and Colonel O'Shea, barely sixty men on inferior horses, held up Cobham's and Kerr's four hundred dragoons, who had attempted to ride round the enclosure and force their way through a breach. With a few followers and part of the Fitzjames Horse, Charles escaped from the field to begin his adventures in the Outer Isles and on the west coast before escaping to France.

The battle was over but Cumberland's men gave no quarter and few escaped. Those that were wounded were shot on the spot or rounded up and placed in prison ships. The future conqueror of Quebec, Wolfe, who was Hawley's brigade major, refused to stomach such barbarity and was reprimanded by the Duke. Major Macbean, a Jacobite, who was overtaken in the retreat, is supposed to have cut down twelve dragoons before being trampled down by others. Another Highlander, Rob Mor MacGillivray, picked up a tram of a cart and knocked down seven men before he was shot. A spectator, Alexander Munro, was chased by a dragoon but managed to kill him in self defence before escaping. The Jacobite losses were about two hundred on the field, but around two thousand including those killed in cold blood afterwards and in the subsequent pursuit. The Hanoverians lost three hundred and sixty-four. The cruel harrying of the glens that followed horrified the nation. 'Nothing like his measures had been known,' said Andrew Lang, 'since the cruelties of Henry VIII on the Border.'

Culloden today

The battlefield of Culloden belongs to the National Trust for Scotland and is clearly visible a few miles from Inverness just off the A9.

In 1984 a visitor centre was opened by Colonel Donald Cameron of Lochiel, twenty-sixth Chief of the Clan Cameron. The centre has a bookshop, a reading room with a selection of books on the Jacobites, a circular display room with drawings of the battle and the aftermath and a video cinema seating fifty people, as well as a restaurant. Leanach Cottage is fenced off and can only be reached from the visitor centre.

The trees have been removed from the battlefield and there are wooden signs showing where cannons and regiments stood. When you leave the main door of the building and turn left you are on the government side (as they marched from Nairn), which is not immediately obvious. The road still cuts off a bit of the battlefield and the wall has not been rebuilt but the tree-clearing is very effective.

INDEX

Printed by C. I. Thomas & Sons (Haverfordwest) Ltd.,
Press Buildings, Merlins Bridge, Haverfordwest.